P9-BIO-731

J

Main

ALL AROUND THE WORLD
IRAN

by Kristine Spanier

Ideas for Parents and Teachers

Pogo Books let children practice reading informational text while introducing them to nonfiction features such as headings, labels, sidebars, maps, and diagrams, as well as a table of contents, glossary, and index.

Carefully leveled text with a strong photo match offers early fluent readers the support they need to succeed.

Before Reading

- "Walk" through the book and point out the various nonfiction features. Ask the student what purpose each feature serves.

- Look at the glossary together. Read and discuss the words.

Read the Book

- Have the child read the book independently.

- Invite him or her to list questions that arise from reading.

After Reading

- Discuss the child's questions. Talk about how he or she might find answers to those questions.

- Prompt the child to think more. Ask: What did you know about Iran before you read this book? What more would you like to learn about this country?

Pogo Books are published by Jump!
5357 Penn Avenue South
Minneapolis, MN 55419
www.jumplibrary.com

Library of Congress Cataloging-in-Publication Data

Names: Spanier, Kristine, author.
Title: Iran / by Kristine Spanier.
Description: Minneapolis, MN : Jump!, Inc., 2020.
Series: All around the world
Includes bibliographical references and index.
Audience: 7-10.
Identifiers: LCCN 2018042625 (print)
LCCN 2018044970 (ebook)
ISBN 9781641286466 (ebook)
ISBN 9781641286442 (hardcover : qalk. paper)
ISBN 9781641286459 (pbk.)
Subjects: LCSH: Iran–Juvenile literature.
Classification: LCC DS254.75 (ebook)
LCC DS254.75 .S635 2019 (print) | DDC 955–dc23
LC record available at https://lccn.loc.gov/2018042625

Editor: Susanne Bushman
Designer: Molly Ballanger

Photo Credits: Andrew V Marcus/Shutterstock, cover; Greentellect Studio/Shutterstock, 1; Pixfiction/Shutterstock, 3; Razak.R/Shutterstock, 4; Ender BAYINDIR/iStock, 5; Germán Vogel/Getty, 6-7; Zurijeta/Shutterstock, 8-9; losmandarinas/Shutterstock, 9; Daniel Karfik/Shutterstock, 10; imageBROKER/SuperStock, 11; ashariat/Getty, 12t; Alibehrendt/Dreamstime, 12b; Rudmer Zwerver/Shutterstock, 12-13t; Budimir Jevtic/Shutterstock, 12-13b; MehmetO/Shutterstock, 14; BornaMir/iStock, 15; Grigvovan/Shutterstock, 16-17; Youshij Yousefzadeh/Shutterstock, 18-19; Christie's Images Ltd./SuperStock, 20; mazzzur/iStock, 20-21; Marquardt_Photography/iStock, 23.

Printed in the United States of America at Corporate Graphics in North Mankato, Minnesota.

TABLE OF CONTENTS

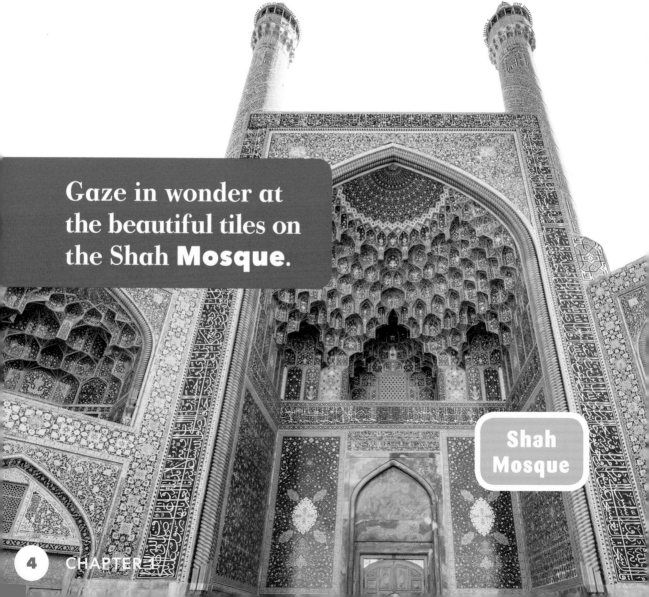

CHAPTER 1

WELCOME TO IRAN!

Gaze in wonder at the beautiful tiles on the Shah **Mosque**.

Shah Mosque

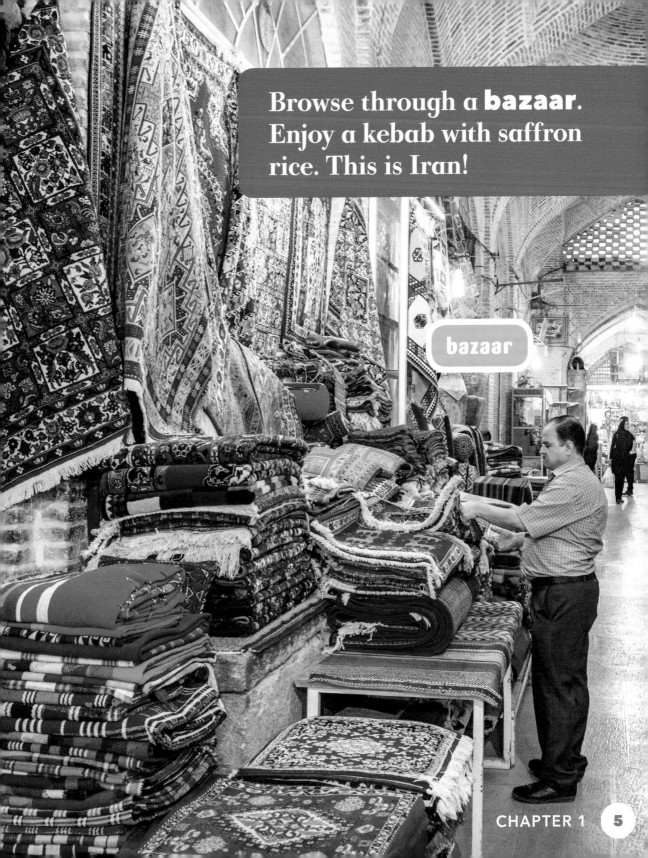

Browse through a **bazaar**. Enjoy a kebab with saffron rice. This is Iran!

bazaar

This area was once called Persia. Tehran is the **capital**. The Azadi Tower is here. It marks an entrance into the city. It was built in 1971. Many special events take place here.

DID YOU KNOW?

Iran has a **president**. But the ayatollah has the most power here. This leader has political and spiritual authority. He makes sure laws fit with Islamic beliefs. Why? Most people here are Muslim.

Azadi
Tower

rice plants ·····▶

Petroleum is a valuable **resource** here. This thick oil is used for fuel. It is also used to make plastics. Ink. Paints. Rubber. Natural gas is found here, too.

Farmers grow wheat, rice, and barley. What else? Tea. Sugar beets. Fruits. Cotton.

◄ · · · · · petroleum

CHAPTER 2

LAND AND ANIMALS

Mount Damavand ····▶

The Zagros Mountains are in the west. The Elburz Mountains are north. Mount Damavand is the highest peak here. This **volcano** last erupted 7,300 years ago!

Desert fills much of the land. Some is covered with sand and stones. Other parts are covered with salt. Why? Water **evaporates** quickly here. It leaves salt behind.

salt

Asiatic cheetah

Eurasian lynx

Persian onager

Persian fallow deer

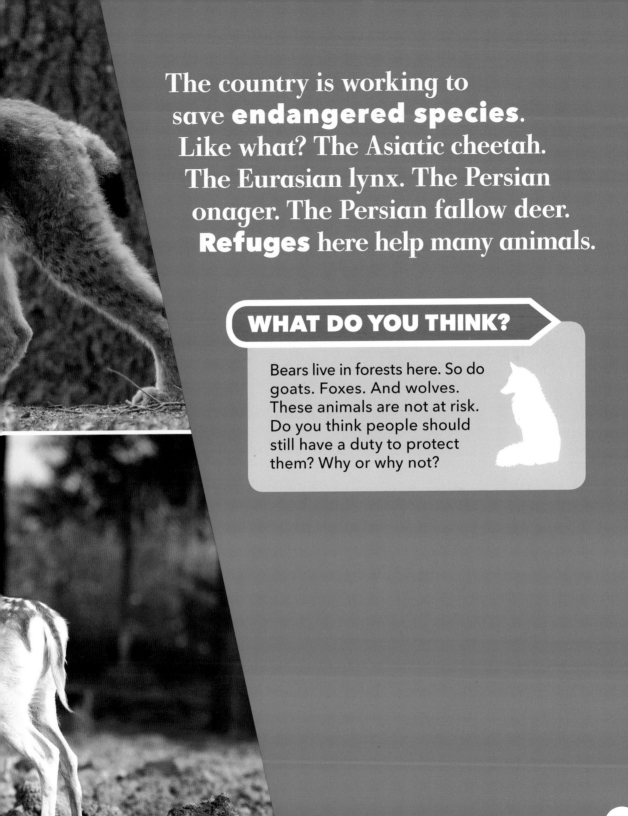

The country is working to save **endangered species**. Like what? The Asiatic cheetah. The Eurasian lynx. The Persian onager. The Persian fallow deer. **Refuges** here help many animals.

WHAT DO YOU THINK?

Bears live in forests here. So do goats. Foxes. And wolves. These animals are not at risk. Do you think people should still have a duty to protect them? Why or why not?

CHAPTER 3
IRAN'S PEOPLE

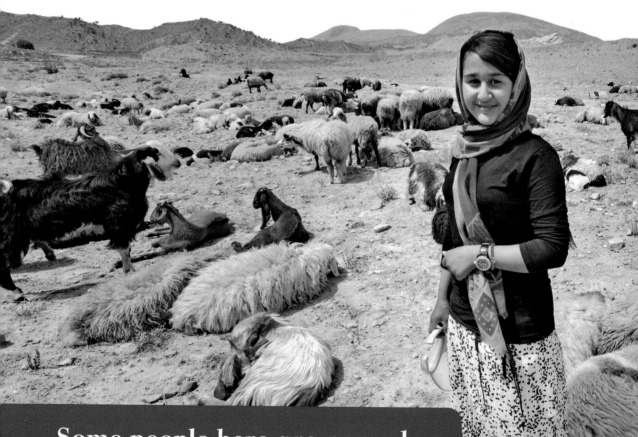

Some people here are nomads. They move from place to place. Why? To find new areas for their **livestock** to graze.

Most people live in cities or towns. Many live in apartments. The streets are crowded with traffic. People use buses or taxis to get around.

Children study Islam in school. What else? Science. Math. Boys complete a **military** course. Why? Most will serve in the military when they are 18 years old.

In **rural** areas, kids may not continue after elementary school. Why not? They may need to help at home. Some work at a family business.

WHAT DO YOU THINK?

In most places here, boys and girls attend separate schools after kindergarten. Would you like to attend a separate school? Why or why not?

Many Islamic holidays are celebrated here. Like what? Ramadan. Eid al-Adha, too. Nowruz is the Persian New Year. It begins on March 21. It marks the start of spring. It lasts four days. Schools close. People visit their friends and family. They might watch fireworks at night.

Nowruz table

TAKE A LOOK!

Certain objects are placed on tables for Nowruz. These objects have special meaning. See some of their meanings below.

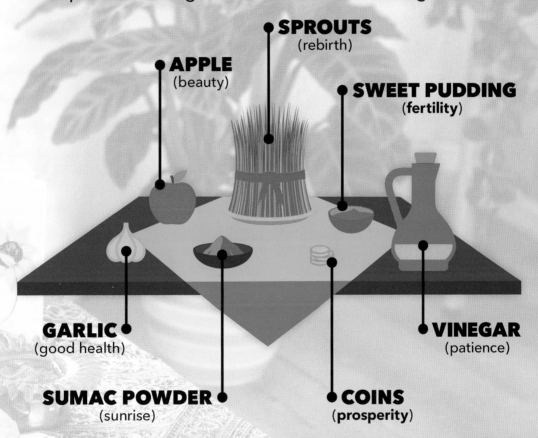

SPROUTS
(rebirth)

APPLE
(beauty)

SWEET PUDDING
(fertility)

GARLIC
(good health)

VINEGAR
(patience)

SUMAC POWDER
(sunrise)

COINS
(prosperity)

People here are known worldwide for their handmade carpets. The designs may be geometric. Or floral. People here also make beautiful **calligraphy**. Or they create silver art objects.

This is a place of great beauty. What would you want to see first?

calligraphy

QUICK FACTS & TOOLS

IRAN

Location: Middle East

Size: 636,372 square miles (1,648,195 square kilometers)

Population: 83,024,745 (July 2018 estimate)

Capital: Tehran

Type of Government: theocratic republic

Language: Persian

Exports: petroleum, fruits, nuts, carpets

Currency: Iranian rial

GLOSSARY

bazaar: A street market.

calligraphy: Artistic, stylized handwriting.

capital: A city where government leaders meet.

endangered species: Plants or animals that are in danger of becoming extinct.

evaporates: Changes into a liquid or gas.

fertility: The ability to grow a lot of crops or have many children.

livestock: Animals that are kept or raised on a farm or ranch.

military: Of or having to do with soldiers, the armed forces, or war.

mosque: A building where Muslims worship.

president: The leader of a country.

prosperity: The condition of succeeding or thriving.

refuges: Places that provide protection or shelter.

resource: Something that is valuable or useful.

rural: Related to the country and country life.

volcano: A mountain with openings through which molten lava, ash, and hot gases erupt.

Iran's currency

INDEX

TO LEARN MORE

Finding more information is as easy as 1, 2, 3.

① **Go to www.factsurfer.com**

② **Enter "Iran" into the search box.**

③ **Click the "Surf" button to see a list of websites.**

FACT SURFER